JAMAICA BAY EDGE ATLAS

JAMAICA BAY REFERENCE LIBRARY 01

JAMAICA BAY EDGE ATLAS

STRUCTURES OF COASTAL RESILIENCE

Jamaica Bay Team
Spitzer School of Architecture
The City College of New York

Catherine Seavitt Nordenson, editor
Associate Professor of Landscape Architecture

Kjirsten Alexander
Research Associate

Danae Alessi
Research Associate

Eli Sands
Research Assistant

JAMAICA BAY REFERENCE LIBRARY
REF 01 Jamaica Bay Edge Atlas

ISBN 978-1-942900-17-7

COPYRIGHT

CONTACT
Catherine Seavitt Nordenson
cseavittnordenson@ccny.cuny.edu
www.structuresofcoastalresilience.org

SCR Jamaica Bay Team
The City College of New York
Spitzer School of Architecture
Program in Landscape Architecture, Room 2M24A
141 Convent Avenue New York, New York 10031

COVER
Aerial imagery tiles, SCR Jamaica Bay study area.

supported by

   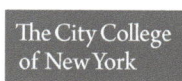

A1 B1 C1 D1 E1 F1 G1 H1 I1

A2 B2 C2 D2 E2 F2 G2 H2 I2

A3 B3 C3 D3 E3 G3 H3 I3

A4 B4 C4 D4 E4 F4 G4 H4 I4

A5 B5 C5 D5 E5 F5 G5 H5 I5

A6 B6 C6 D6 E6 F6 G6 H6 I6

A7 B7 C7 D7 E7 F7 G7 H7 I7

A8 B8 C8 D8 E8 F8 G8 H8 I8

A9 B9 C9 D9 E9 F9 G9 H9 I9

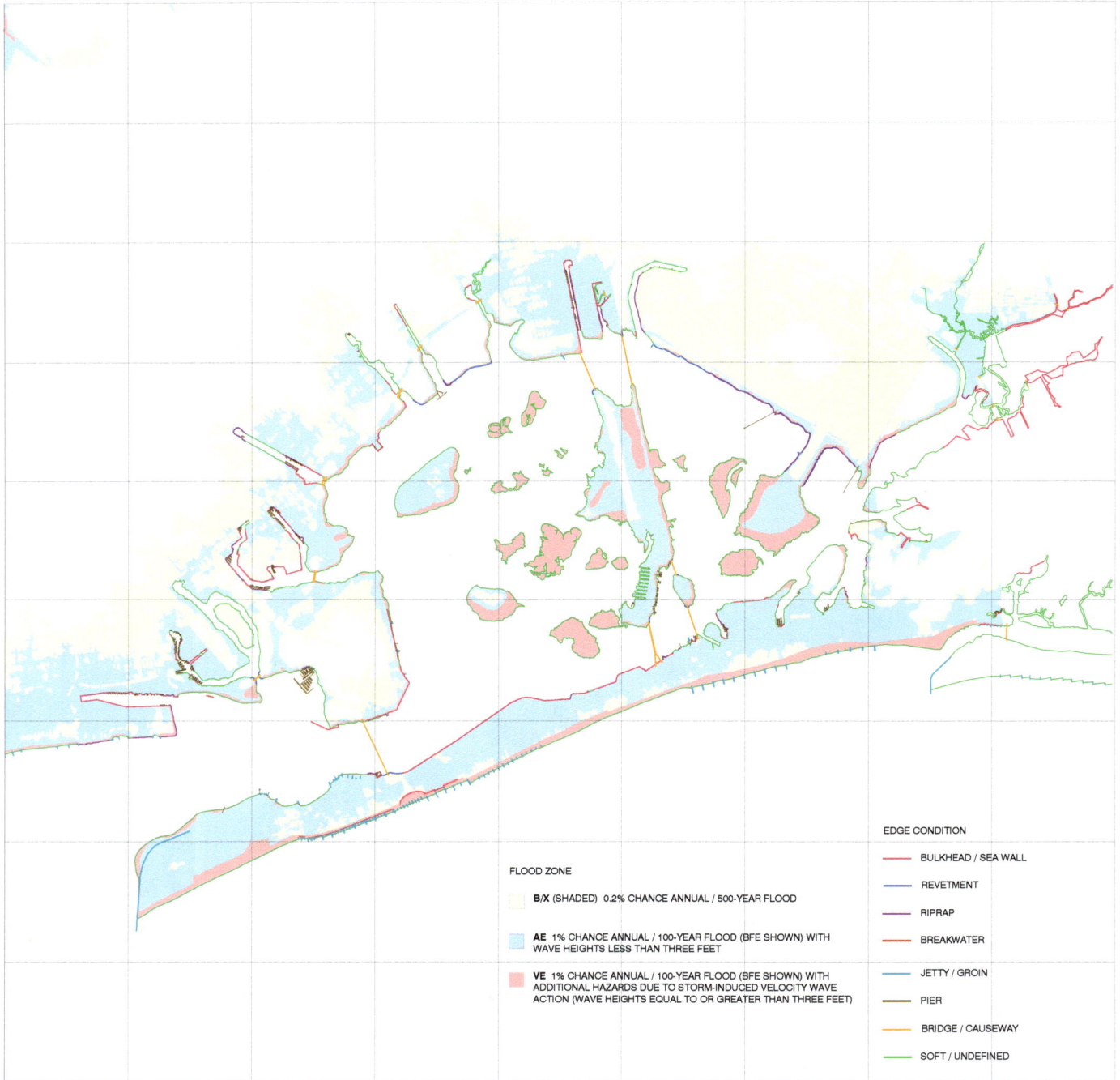

FLOOD ZONE

B/X (SHADED) 0.2% CHANCE ANNUAL / 500-YEAR FLOOD

AE 1% CHANCE ANNUAL / 100-YEAR FLOOD (BFE SHOWN) WITH WAVE HEIGHTS LESS THAN THREE FEET

VE 1% CHANCE ANNUAL / 100-YEAR FLOOD (BFE SHOWN) WITH ADDITIONAL HAZARDS DUE TO STORM-INDUCED VELOCITY WAVE ACTION (WAVE HEIGHTS EQUAL TO OR GREATER THAN THREE FEET)

EDGE CONDITION

BULKHEAD / SEA WALL

REVETMENT

RIPRAP

BREAKWATER

JETTY / GROIN

PIER

BRIDGE / CAUSEWAY

SOFT / UNDEFINED

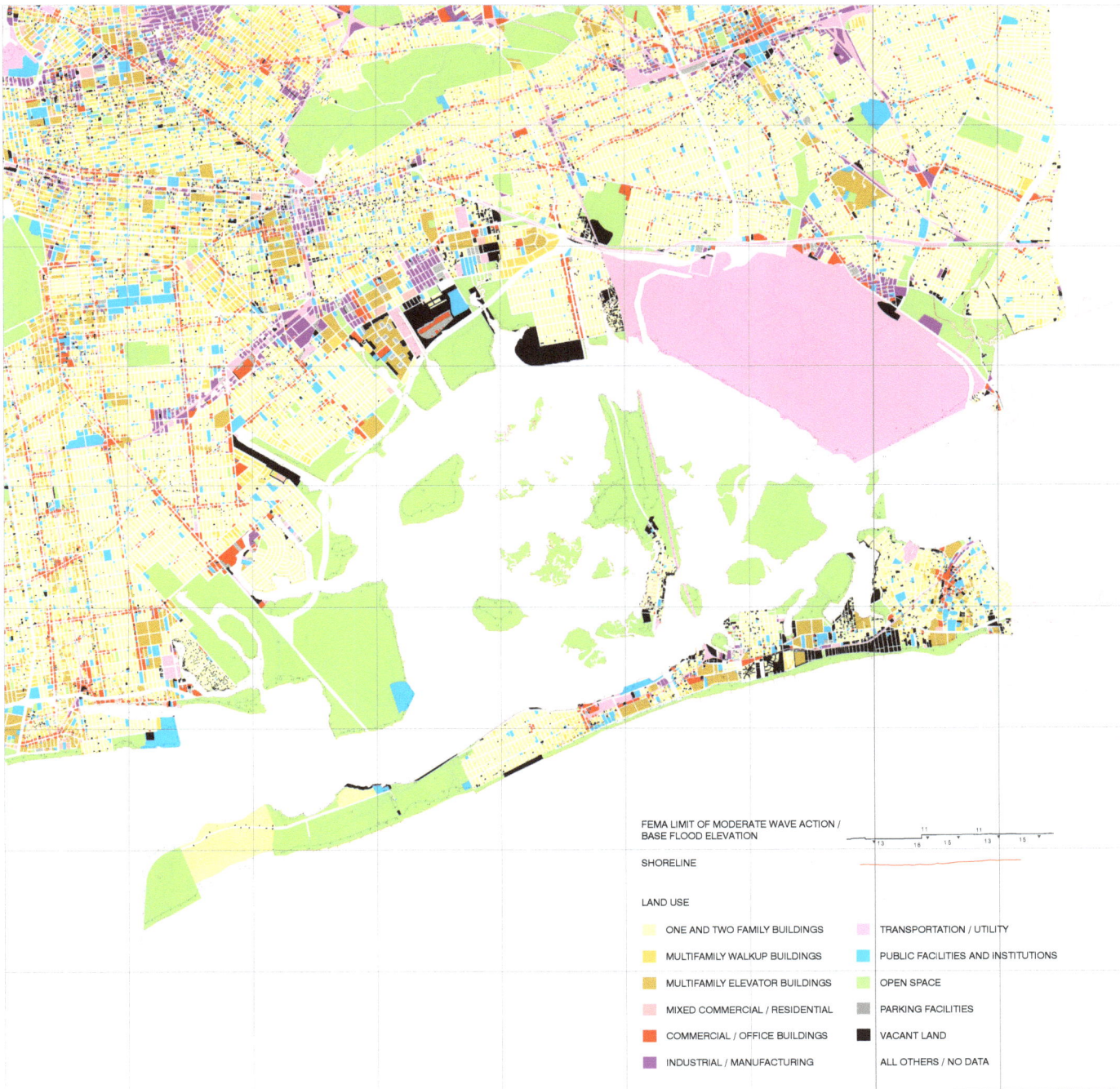

FEMA LIMIT OF MODERATE WAVE ACTION /
BASE FLOOD ELEVATION

SHORELINE

LAND USE

ONE AND TWO FAMILY BUILDINGS

MULTIFAMILY WALKUP BUILDINGS

MULTIFAMILY ELEVATOR BUILDINGS

MIXED COMMERCIAL / RESIDENTIAL

COMMERCIAL / OFFICE BUILDINGS

INDUSTRIAL / MANUFACTURING

TRANSPORTATION / UTILITY

PUBLIC FACILITIES AND INSTITUTIONS

OPEN SPACE

PARKING FACILITIES

VACANT LAND

ALL OTHERS / NO DATA

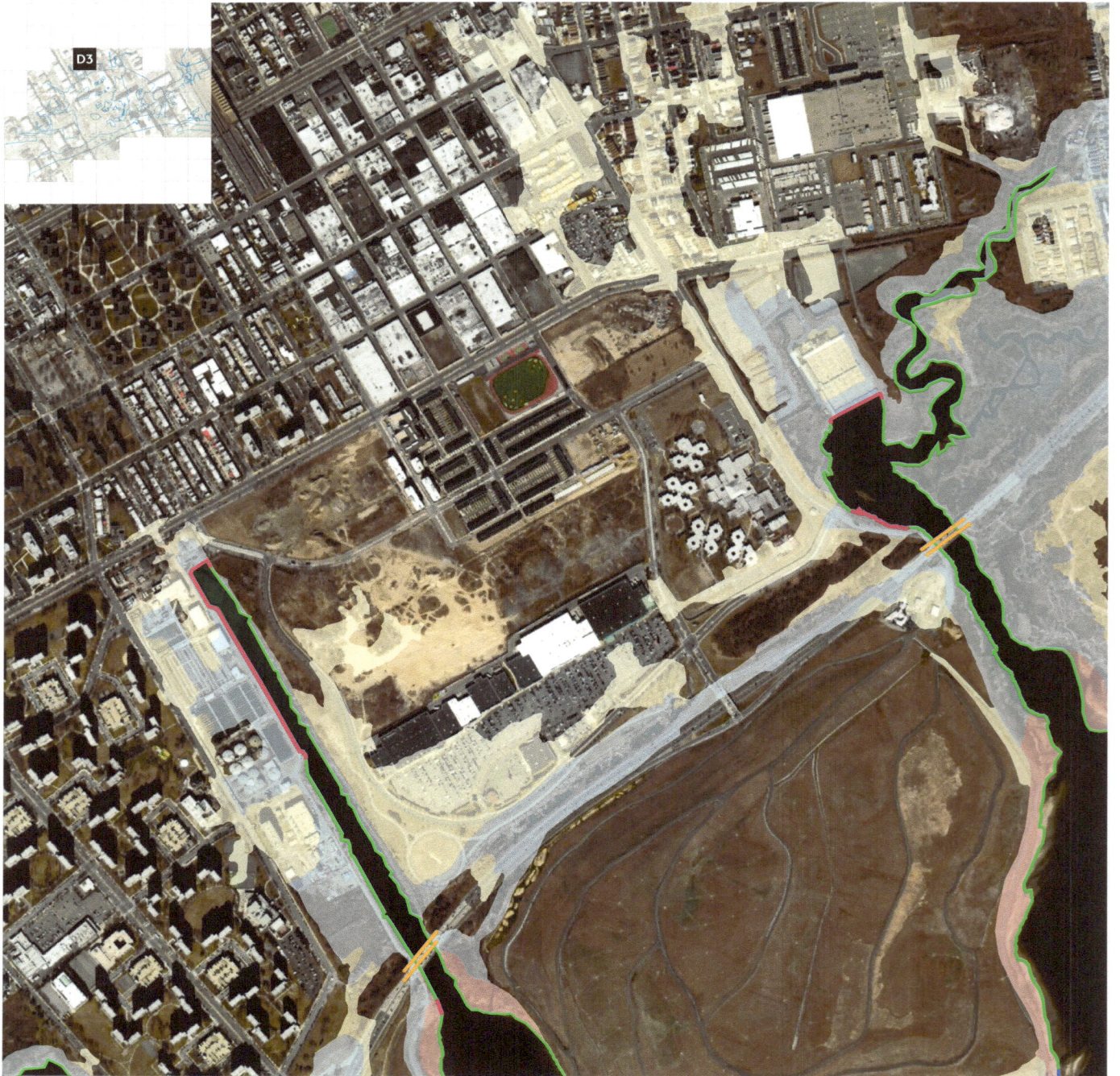

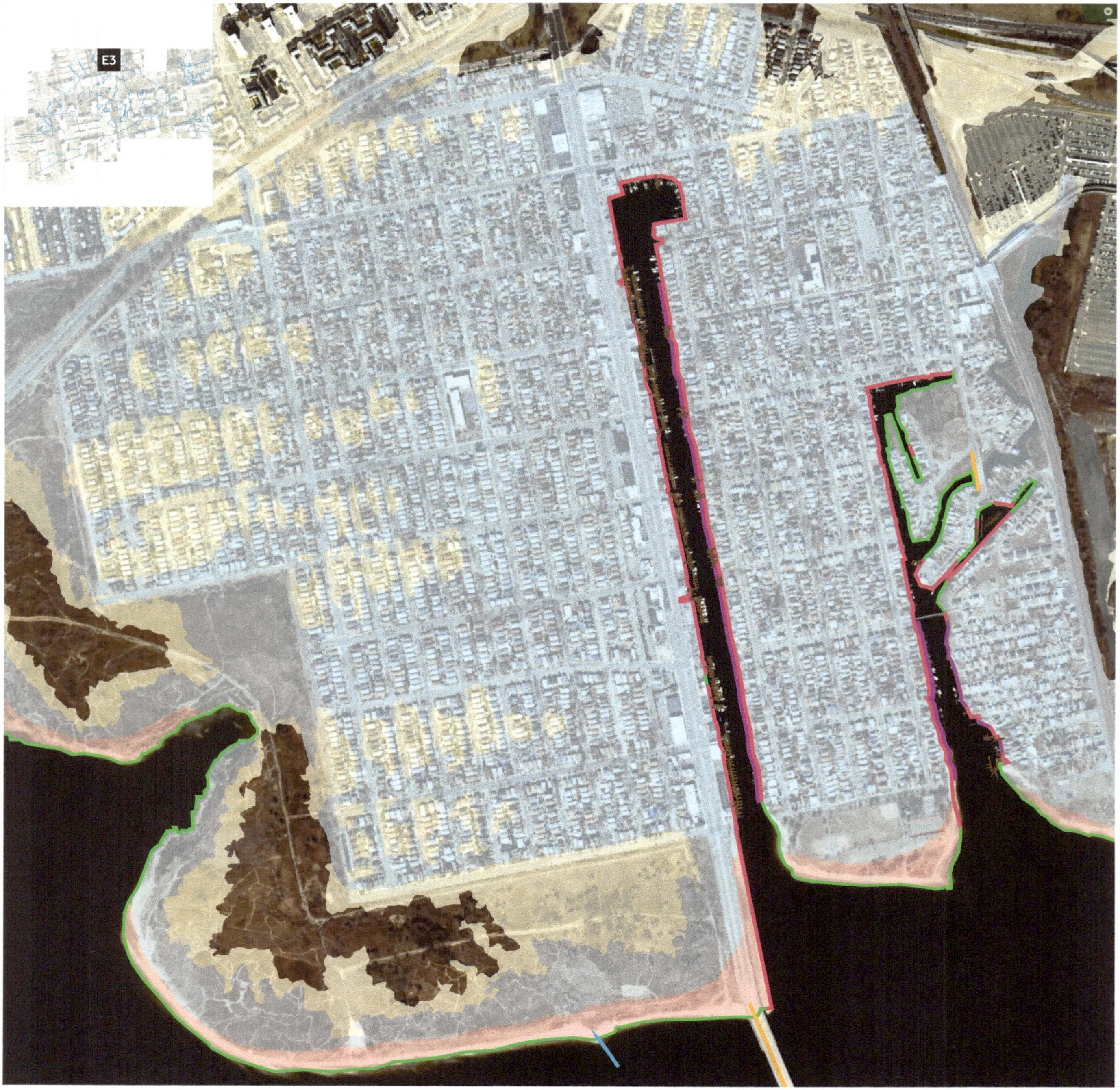
E3

1 0

1 2

1 3

1 1

1 3

12

10

110

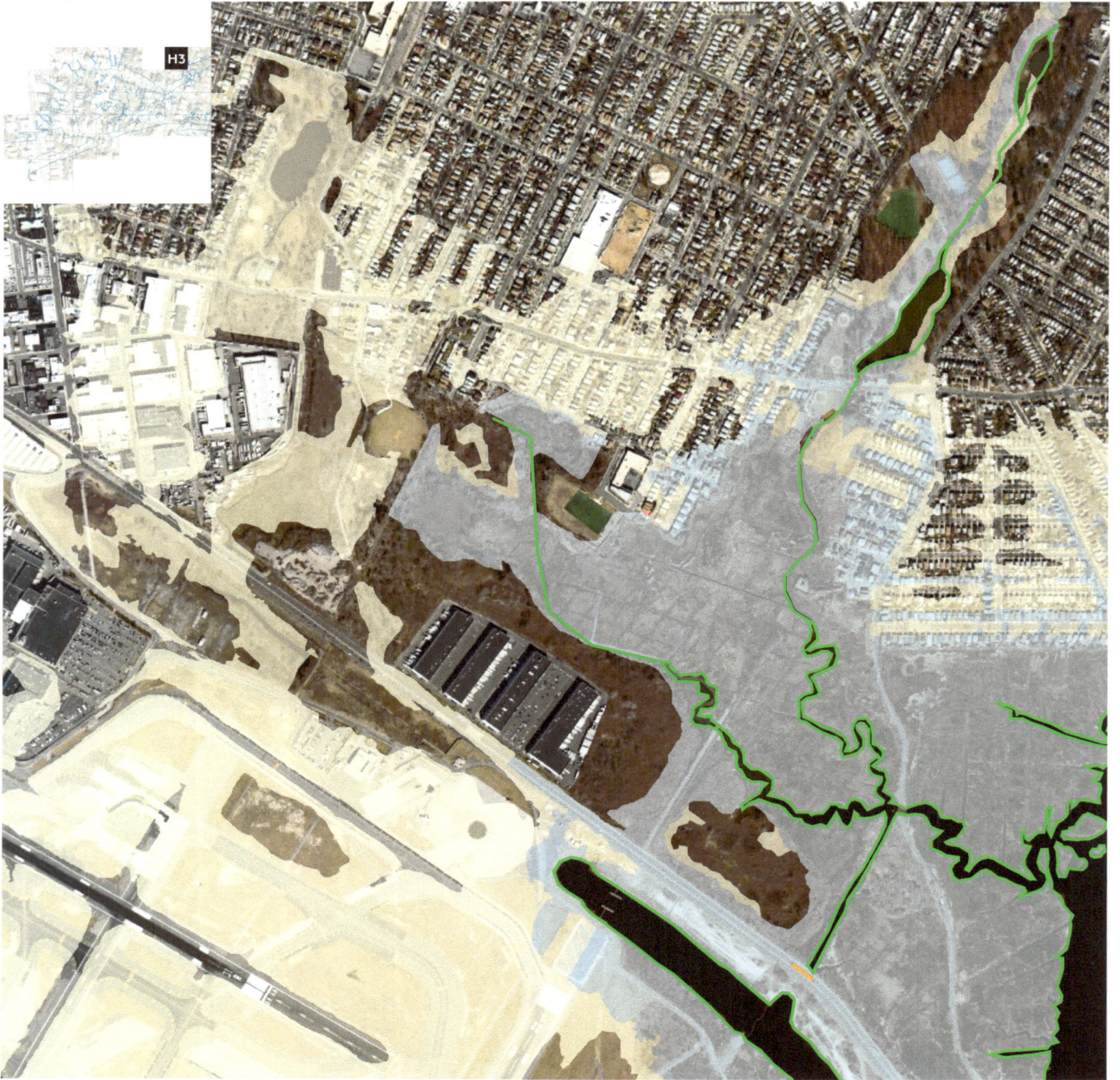

9

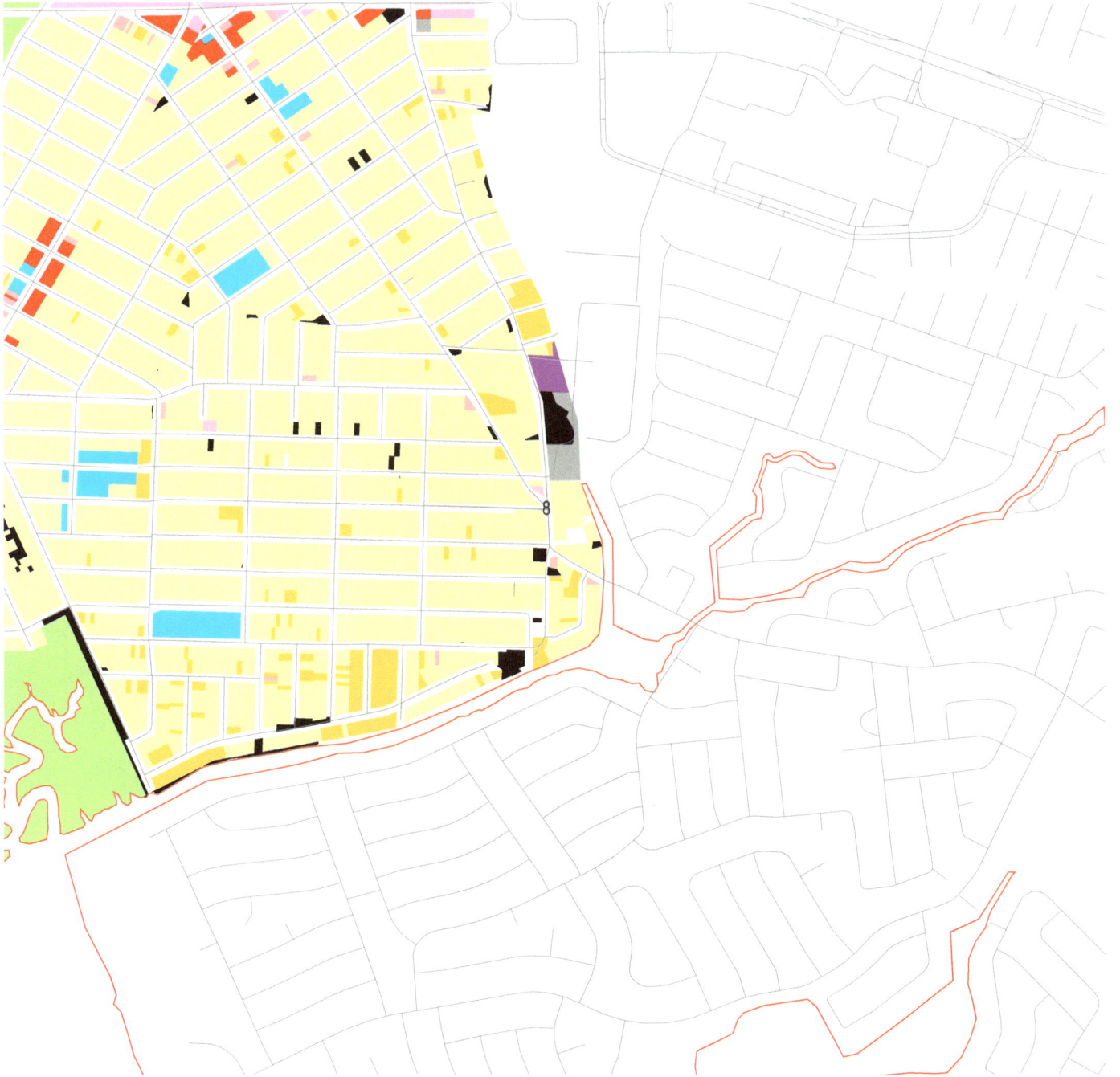

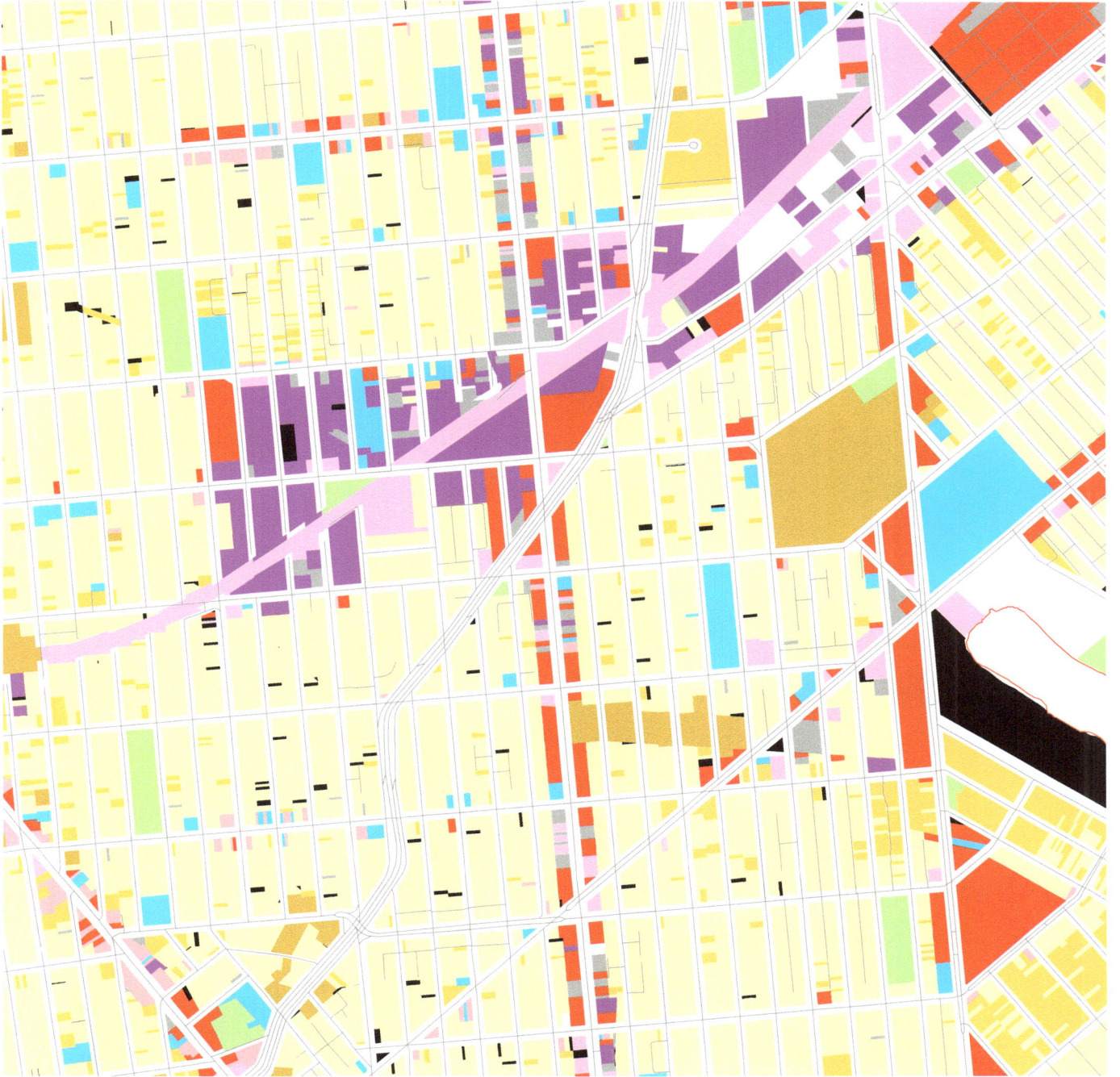

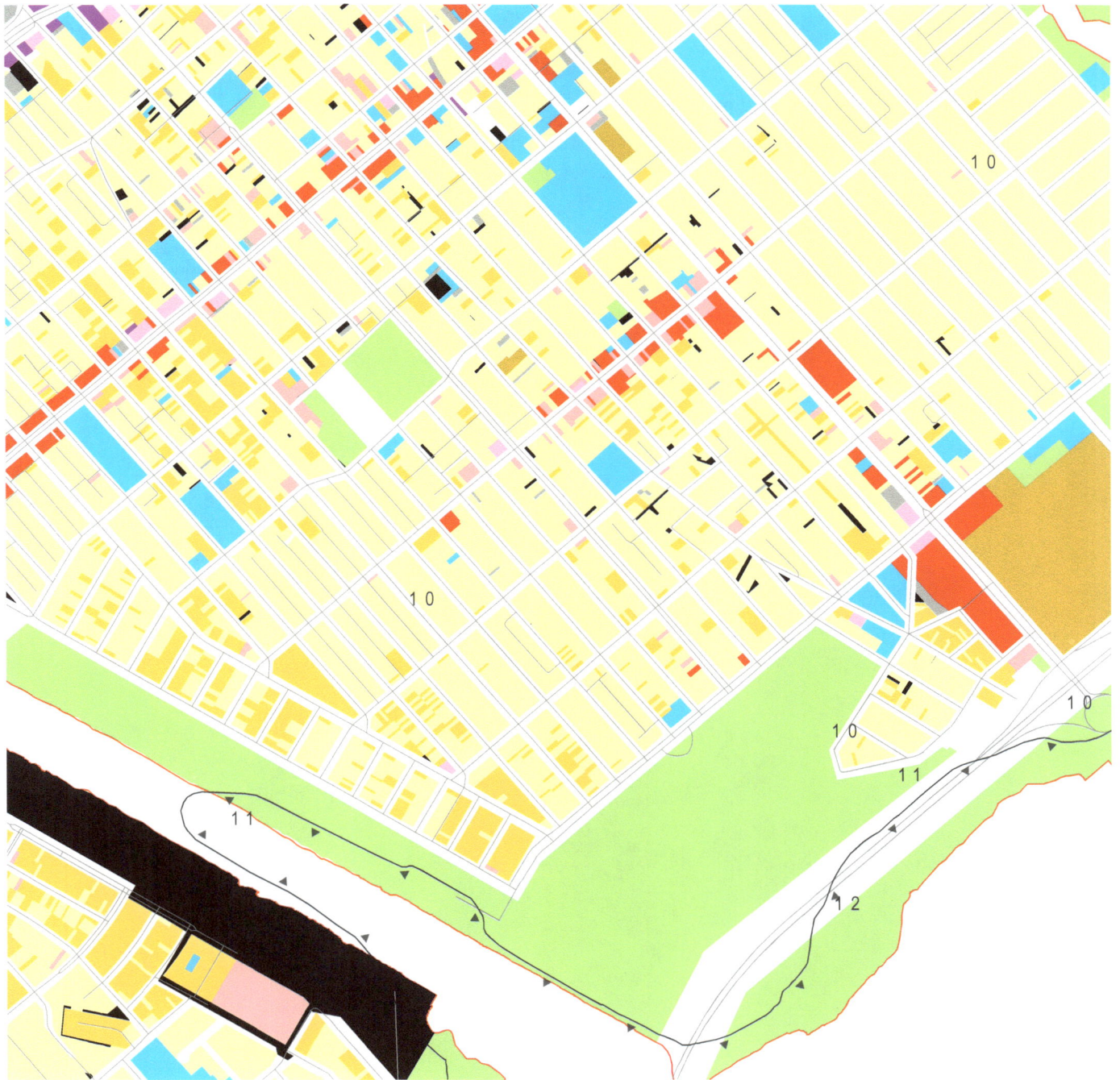

10

10

10

10

11

11

12

1 1

1 0

1 2

1 2

1 2

1 0

1 1

1 2

1 2

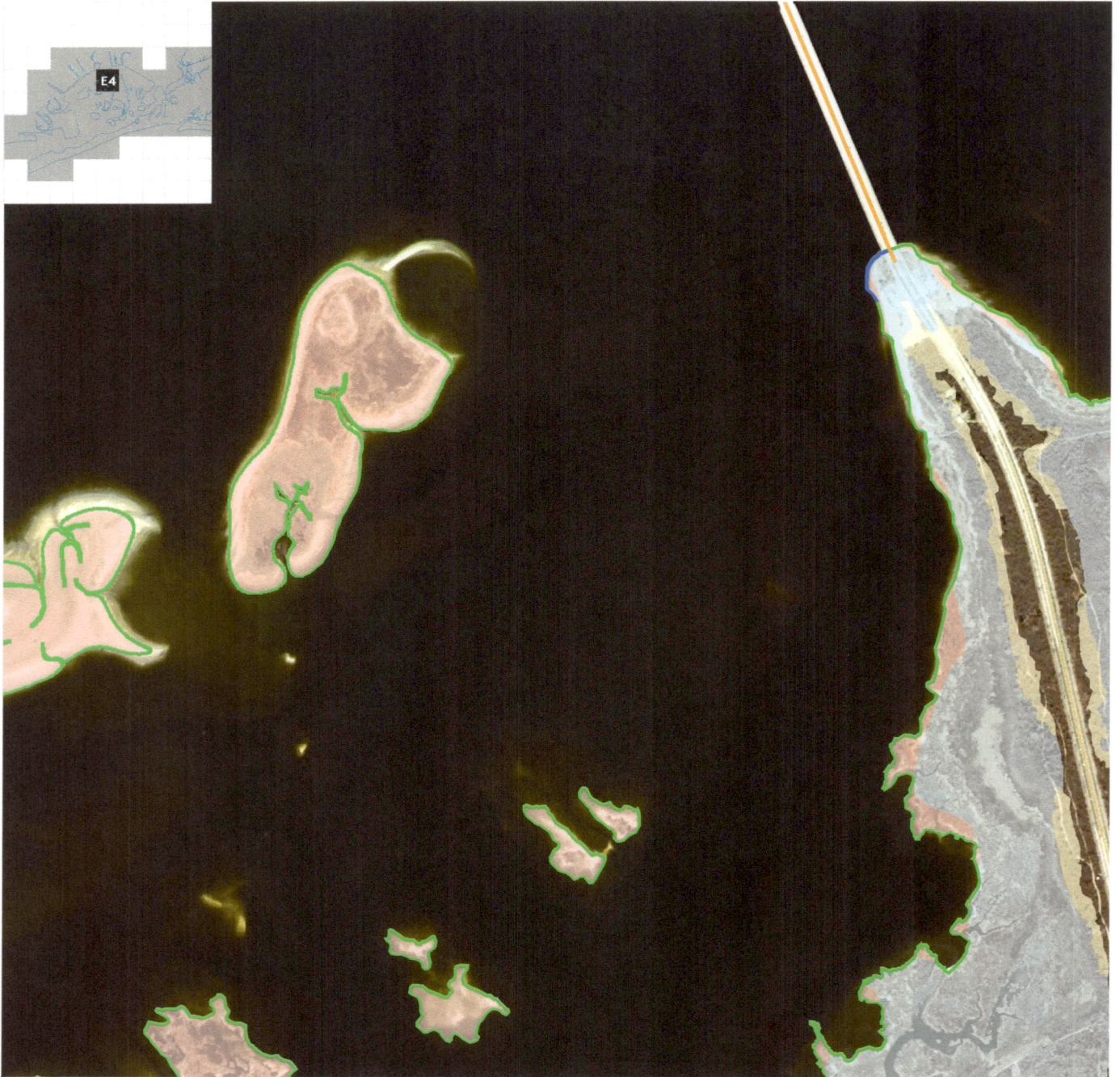

E4

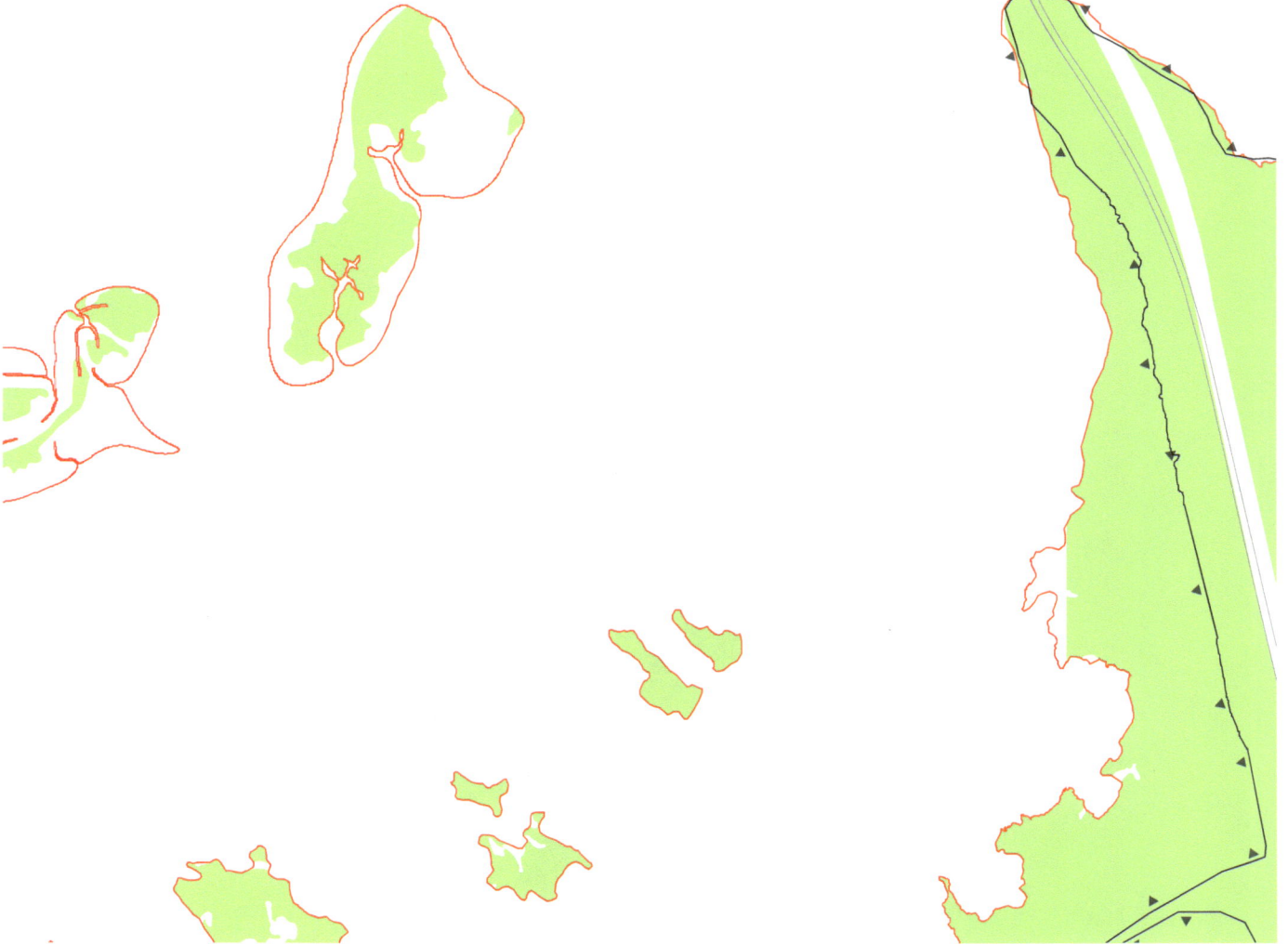

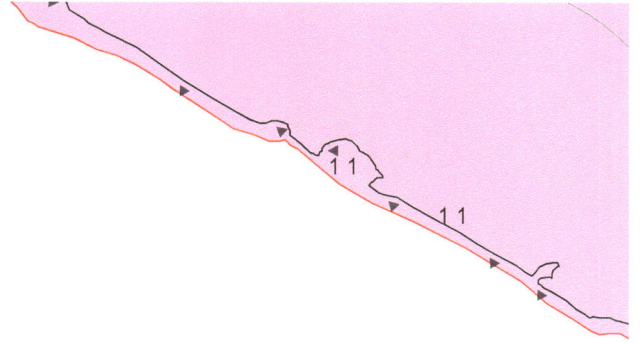

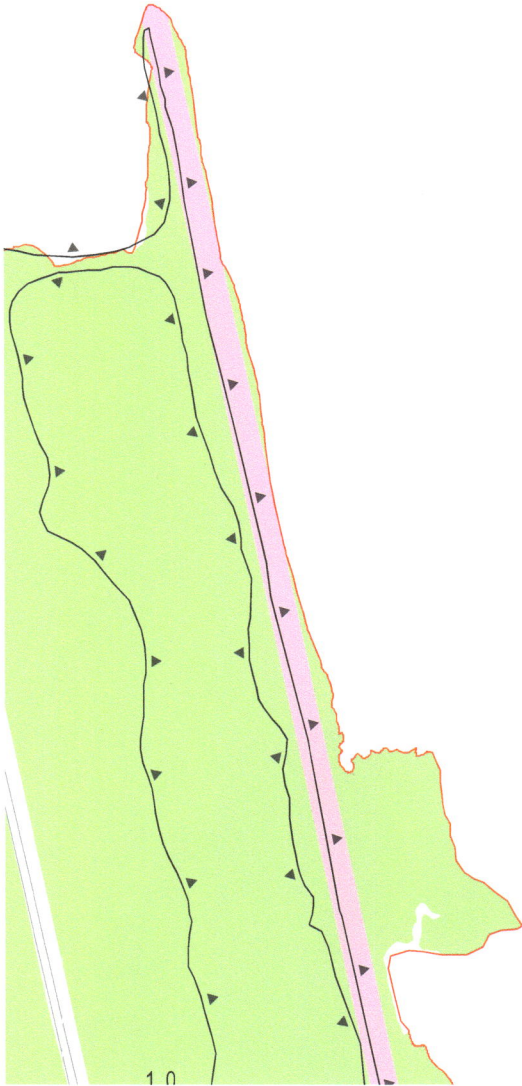

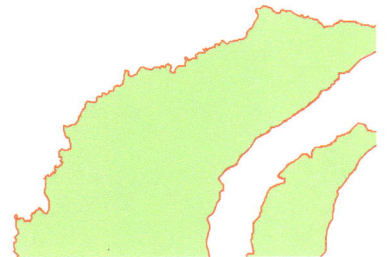

11

11

1 0

G4

1 2

1 1

1 0

1 1

10

9

11

9

10

13

9

14

2

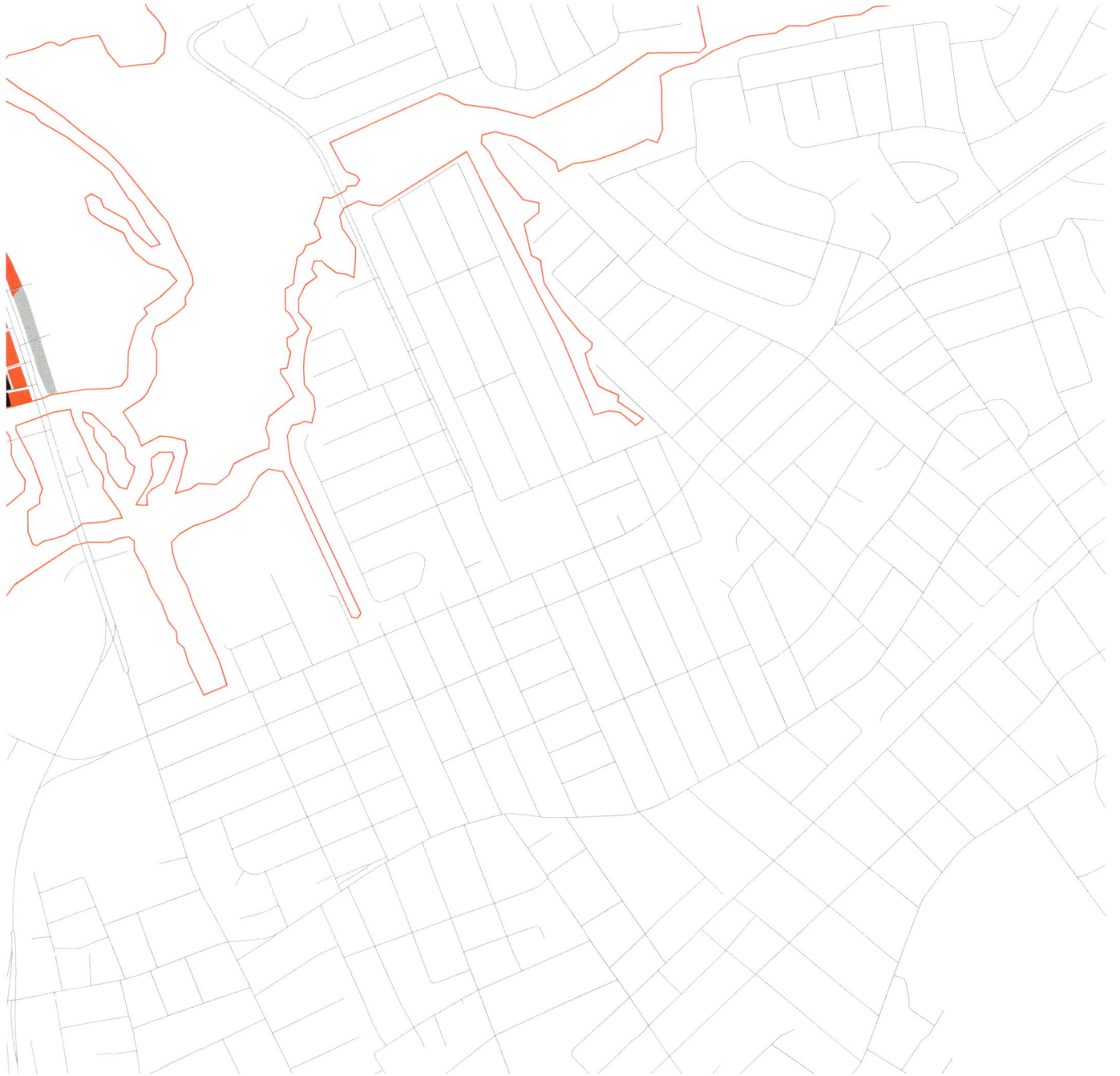

C5

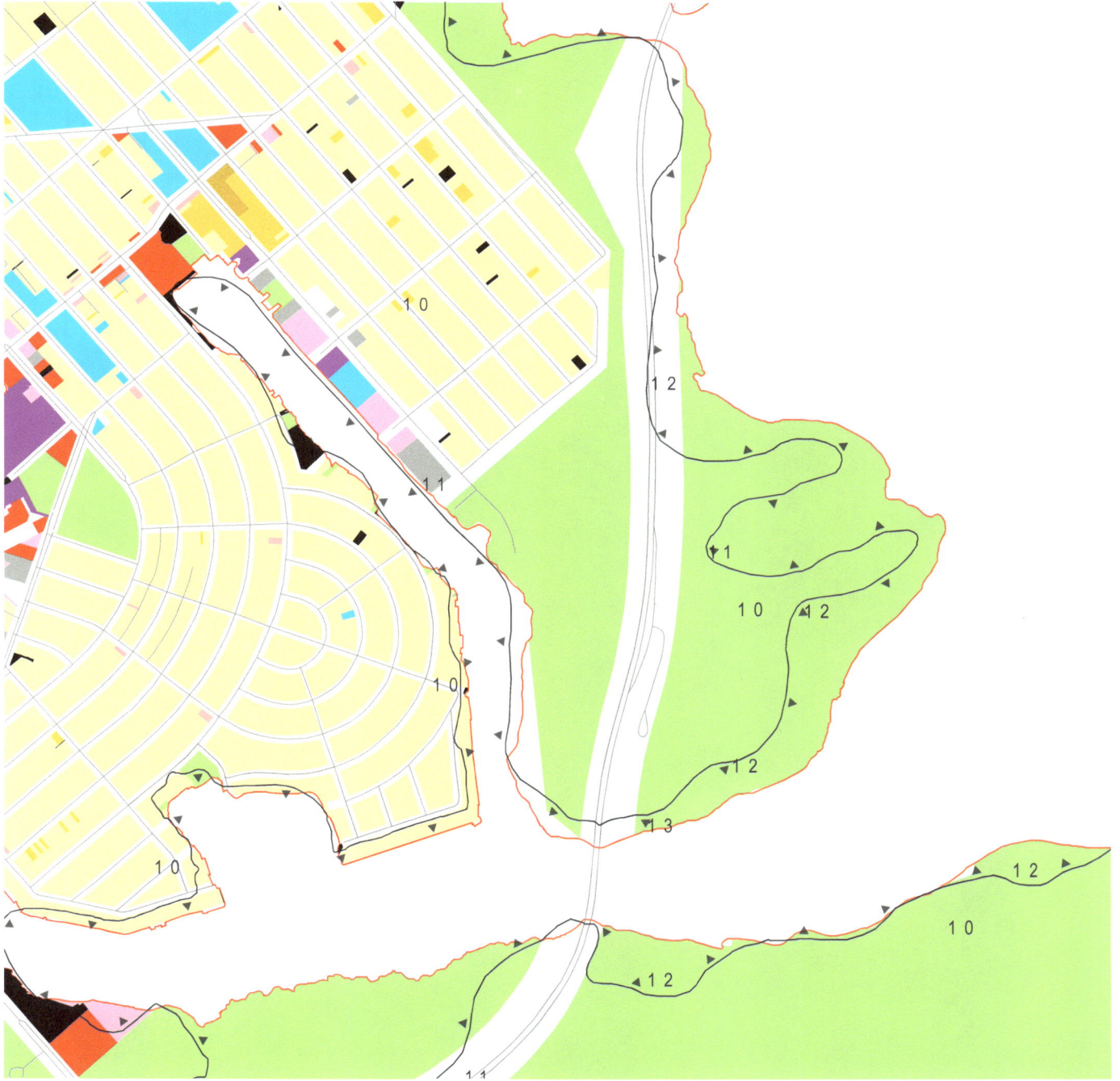

10

12

11

1

10

12

10

12

13

12

10

12

10

11

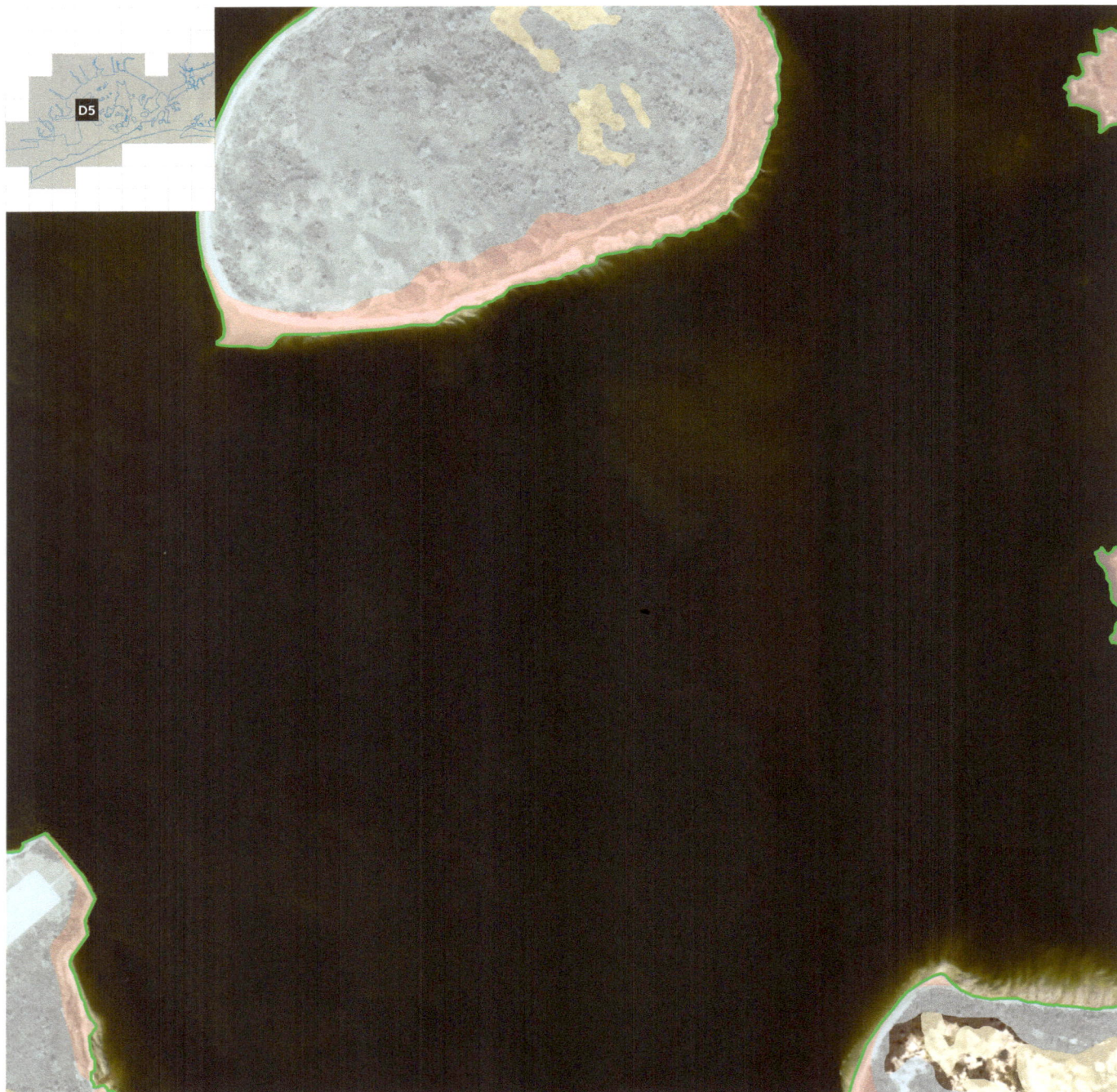

D5

1 0

1 1

1 2

1 2

1 2

1 0

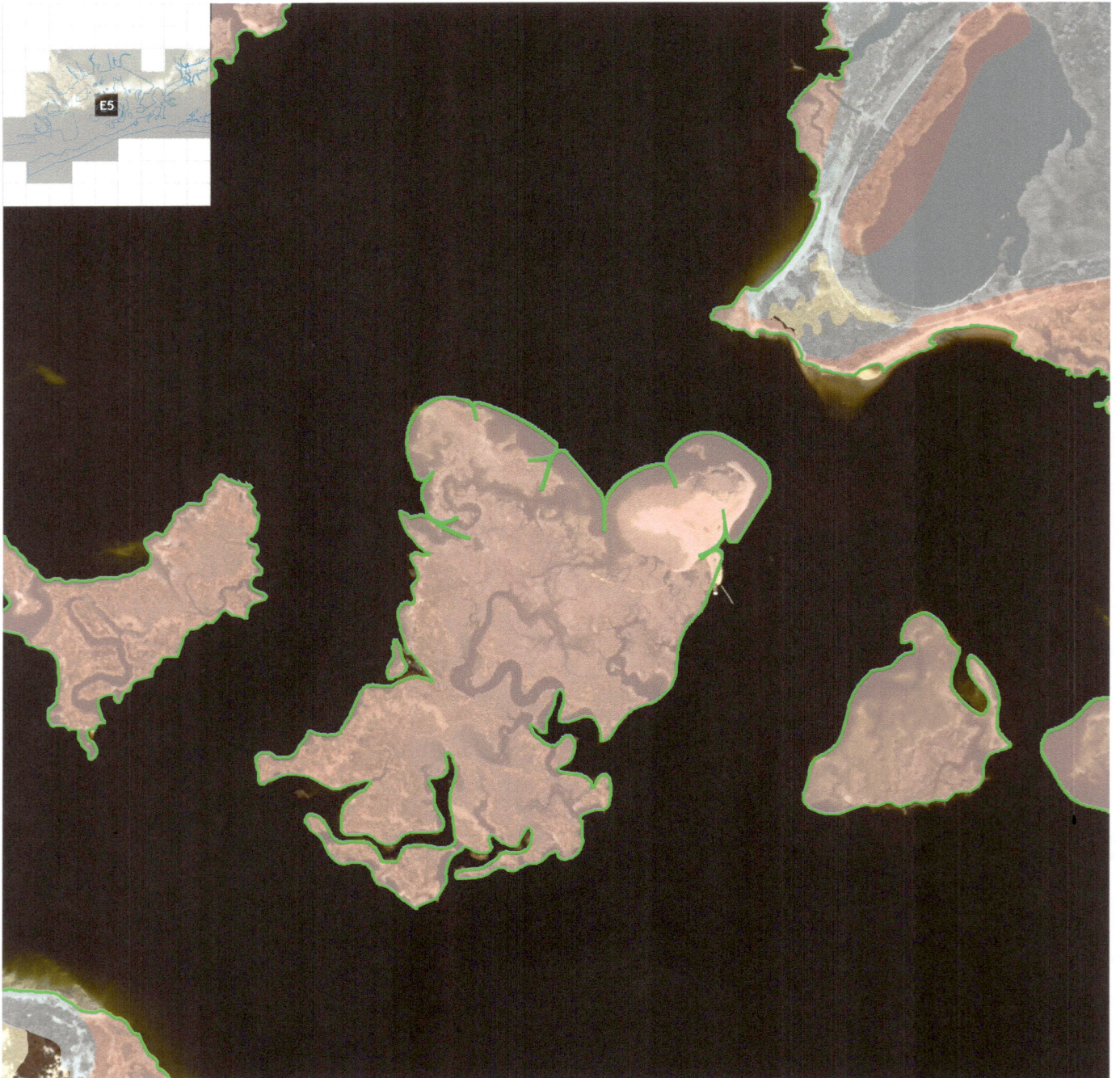

E5

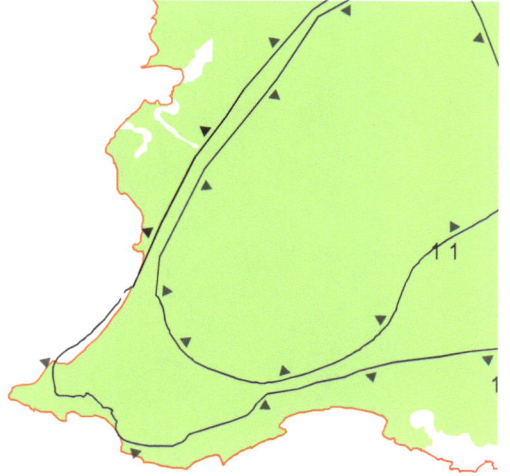

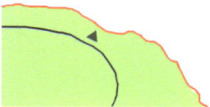

F5

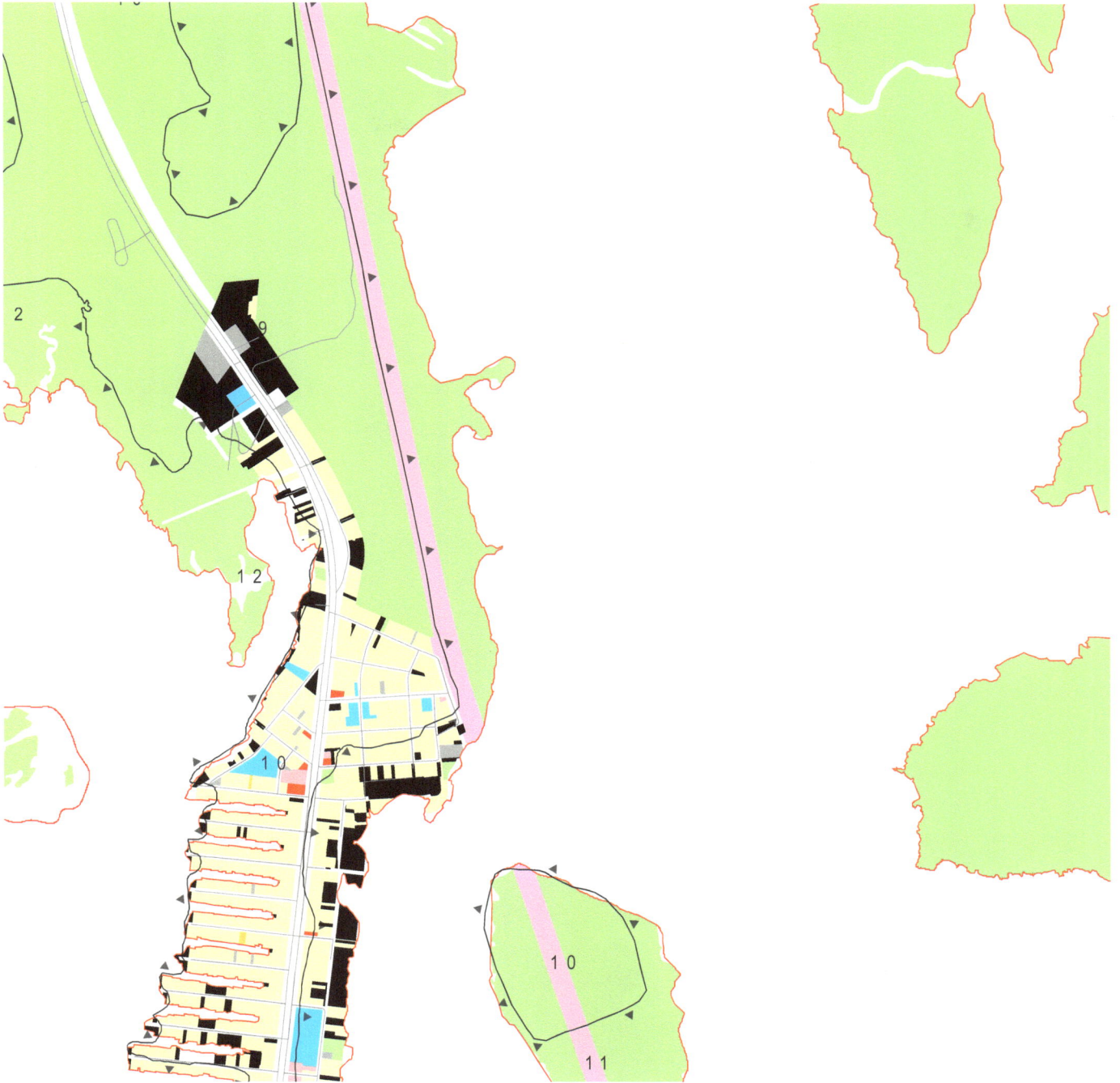

2

9

1 2

1 0

1 0

1 1

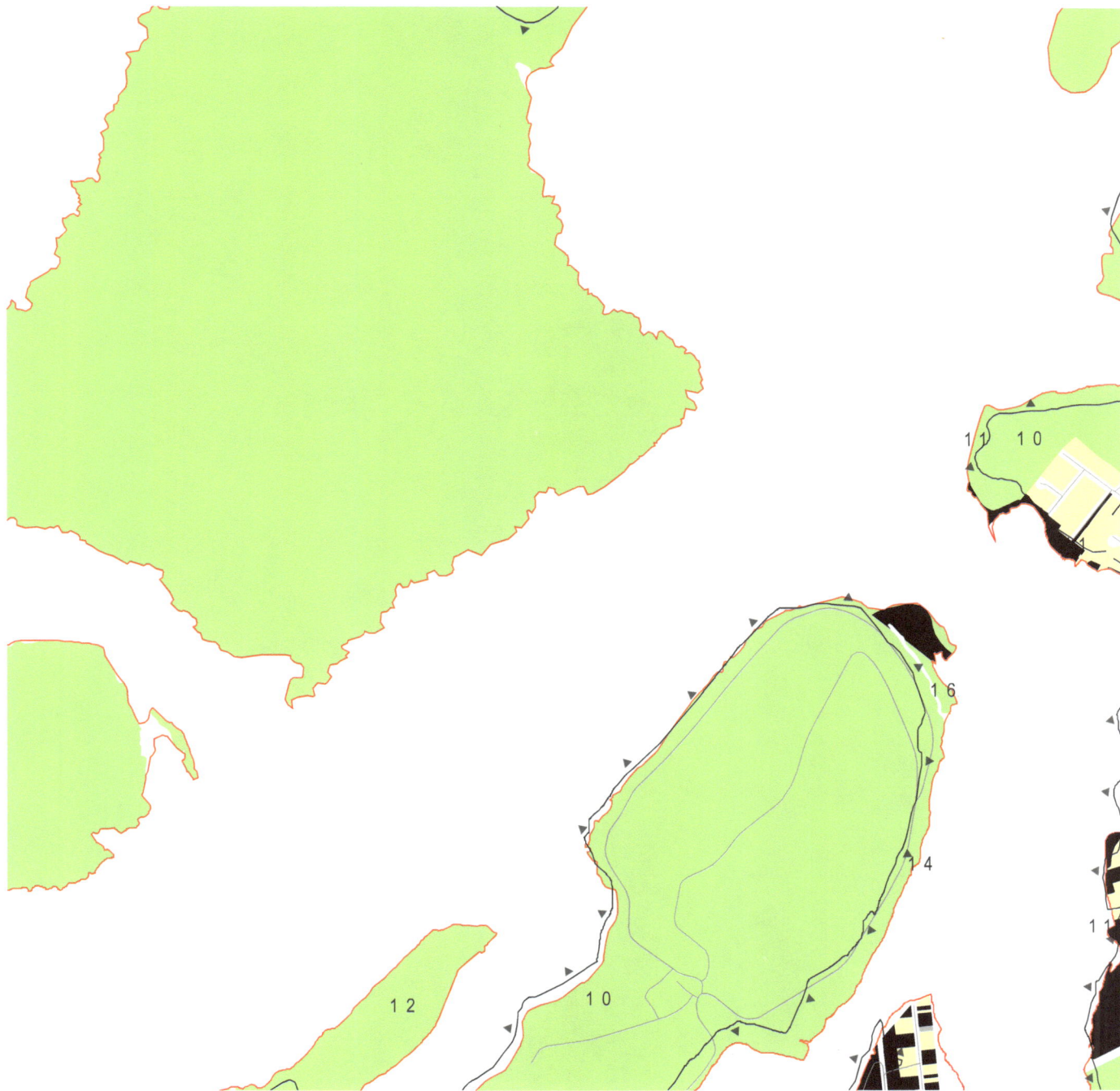

11 10

16

4

12

10

1

H5

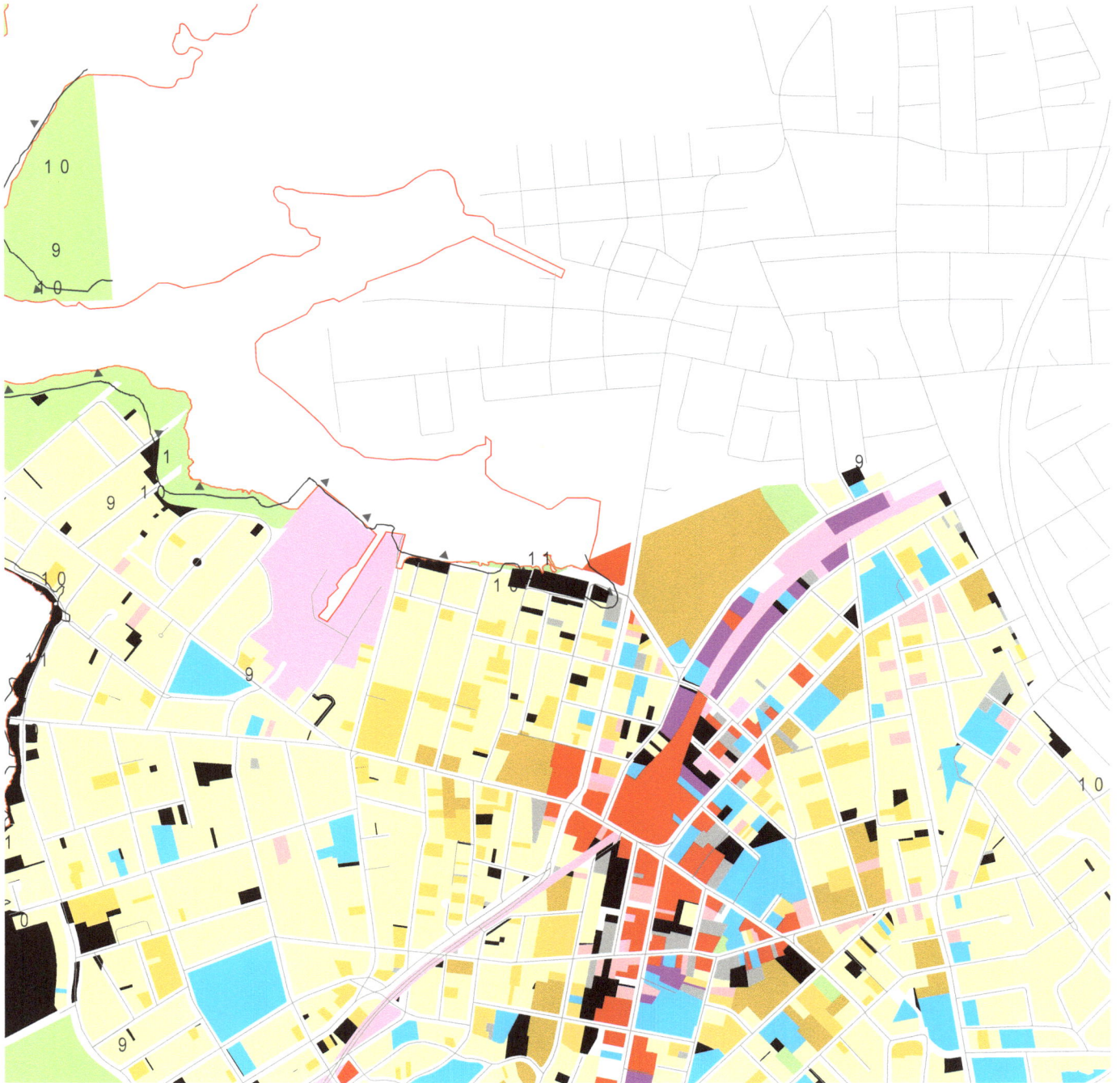

1 0

9

1 0

9 1
1

1 0

1

1 0

1

9

9

1 1

1 0

9

1 0

15

10

10

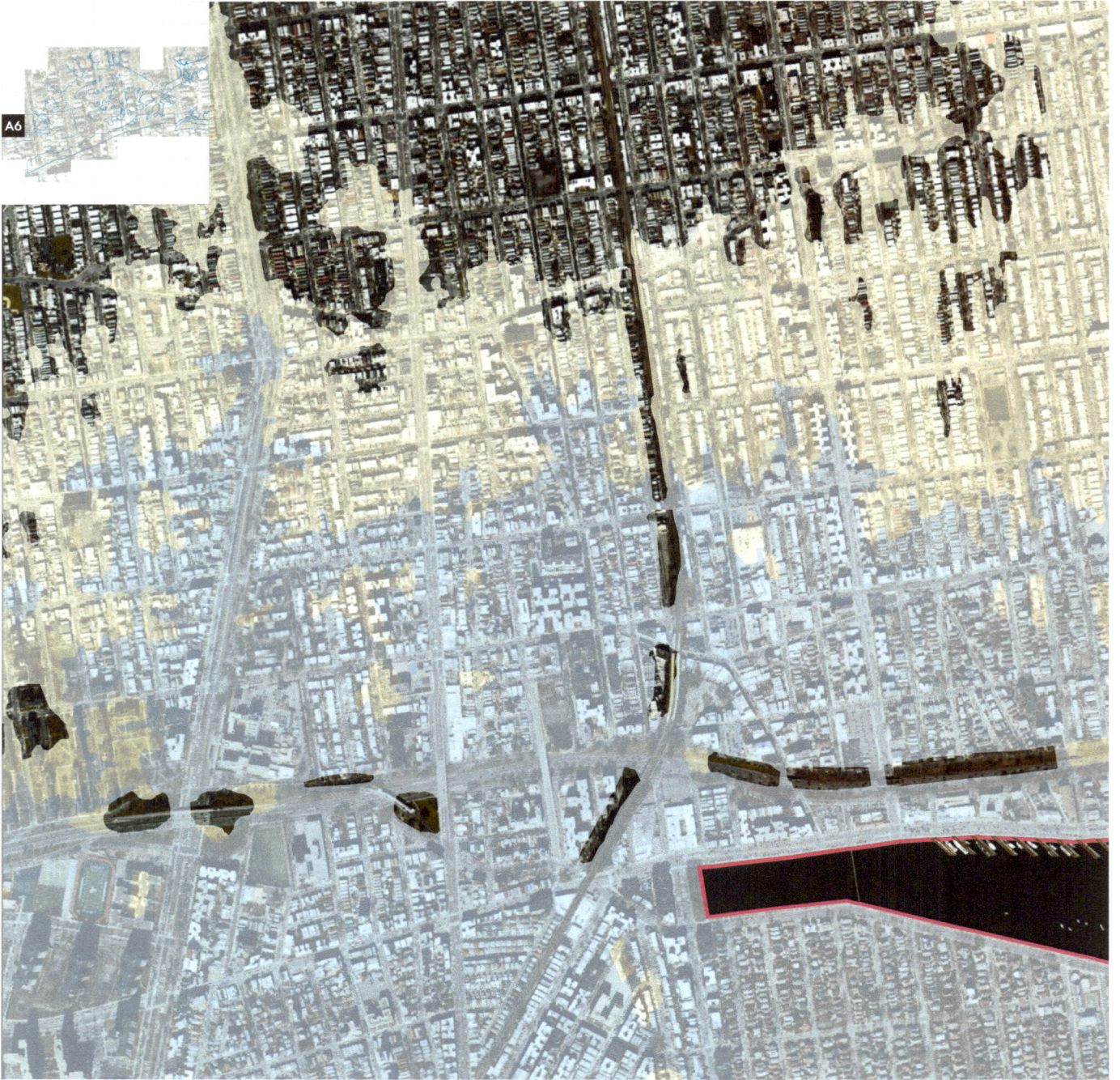

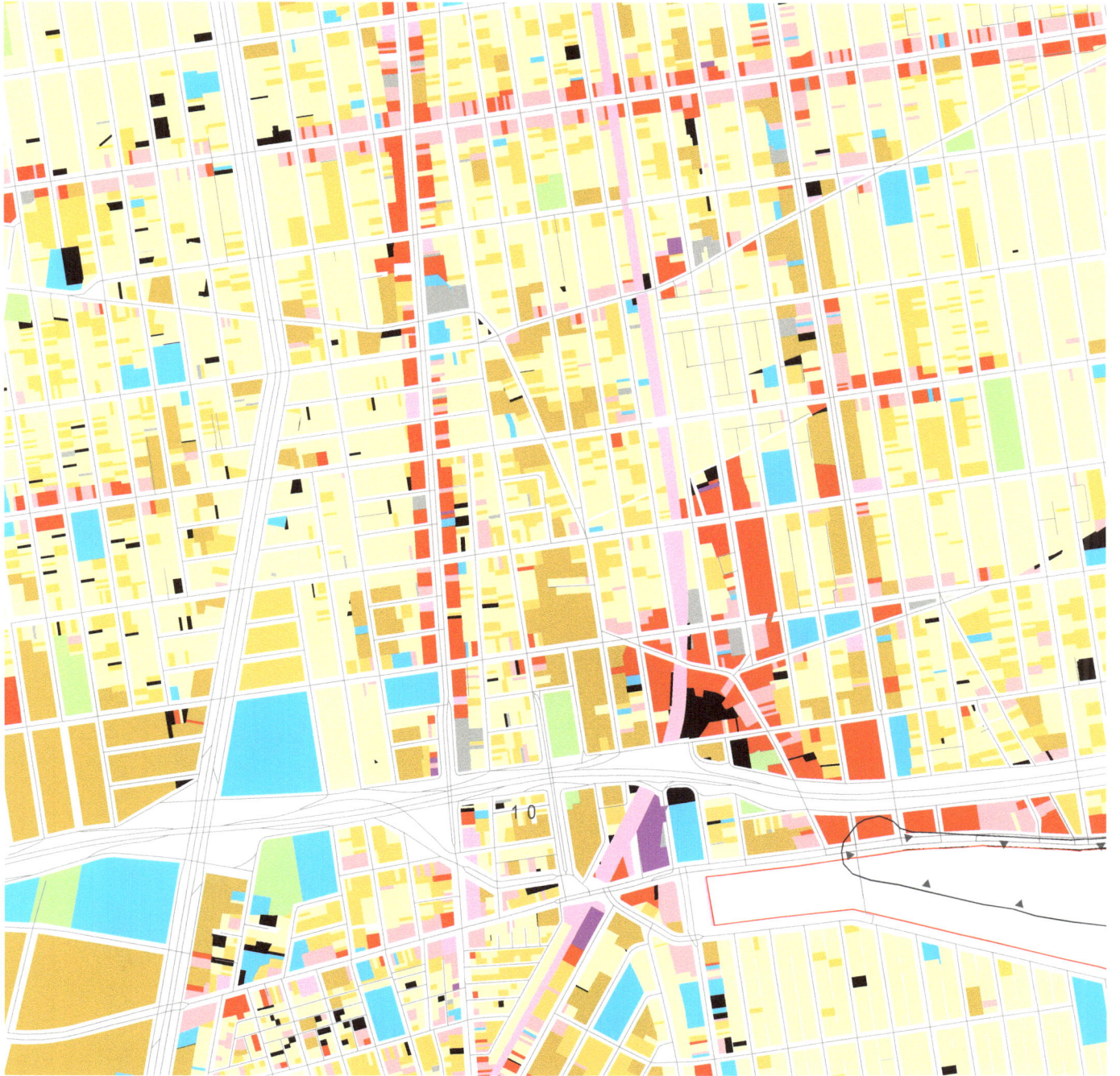

B6

1 0

1 0

2

1 0

1 1

1 2

1 3

1 1

1 2

1 3

1 1

0

1 1

D6

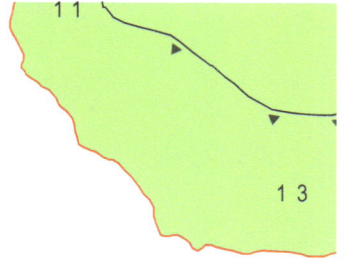

1 1

1 3

1 1

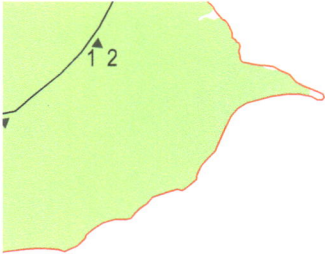

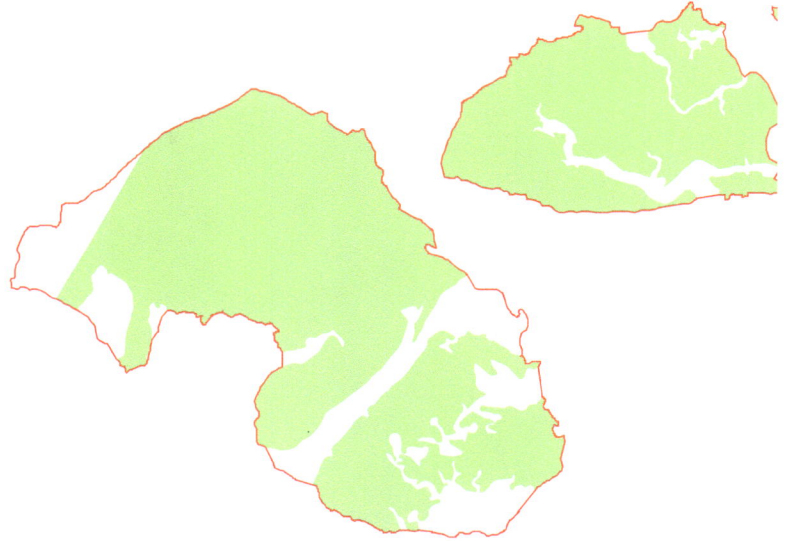

F6

G6

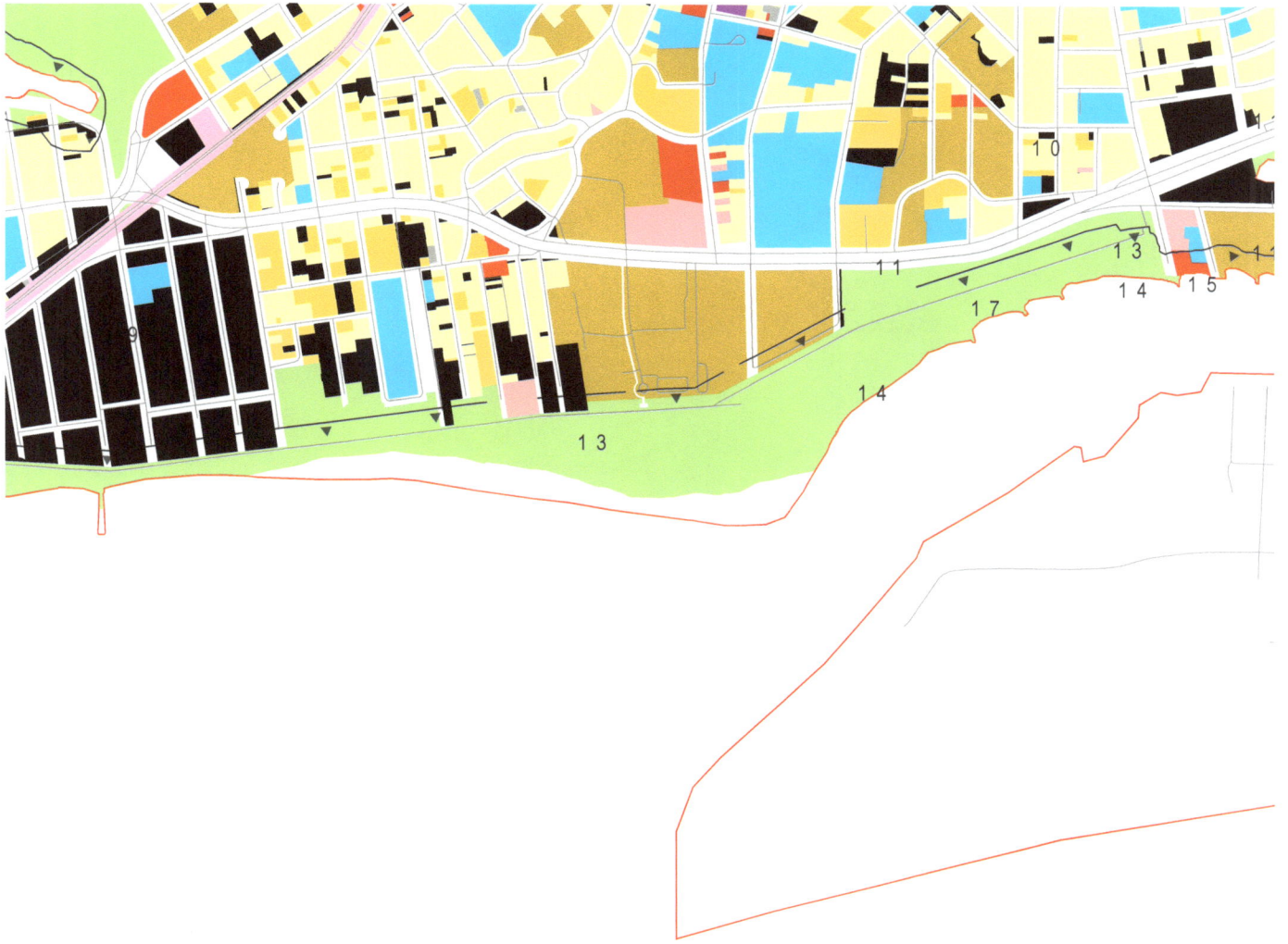

1 3   1 4

A7

B7

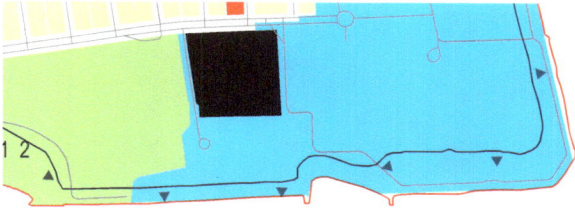

11

10

11

11

11 11 11

11

12

13

11

14

13

14

1 15

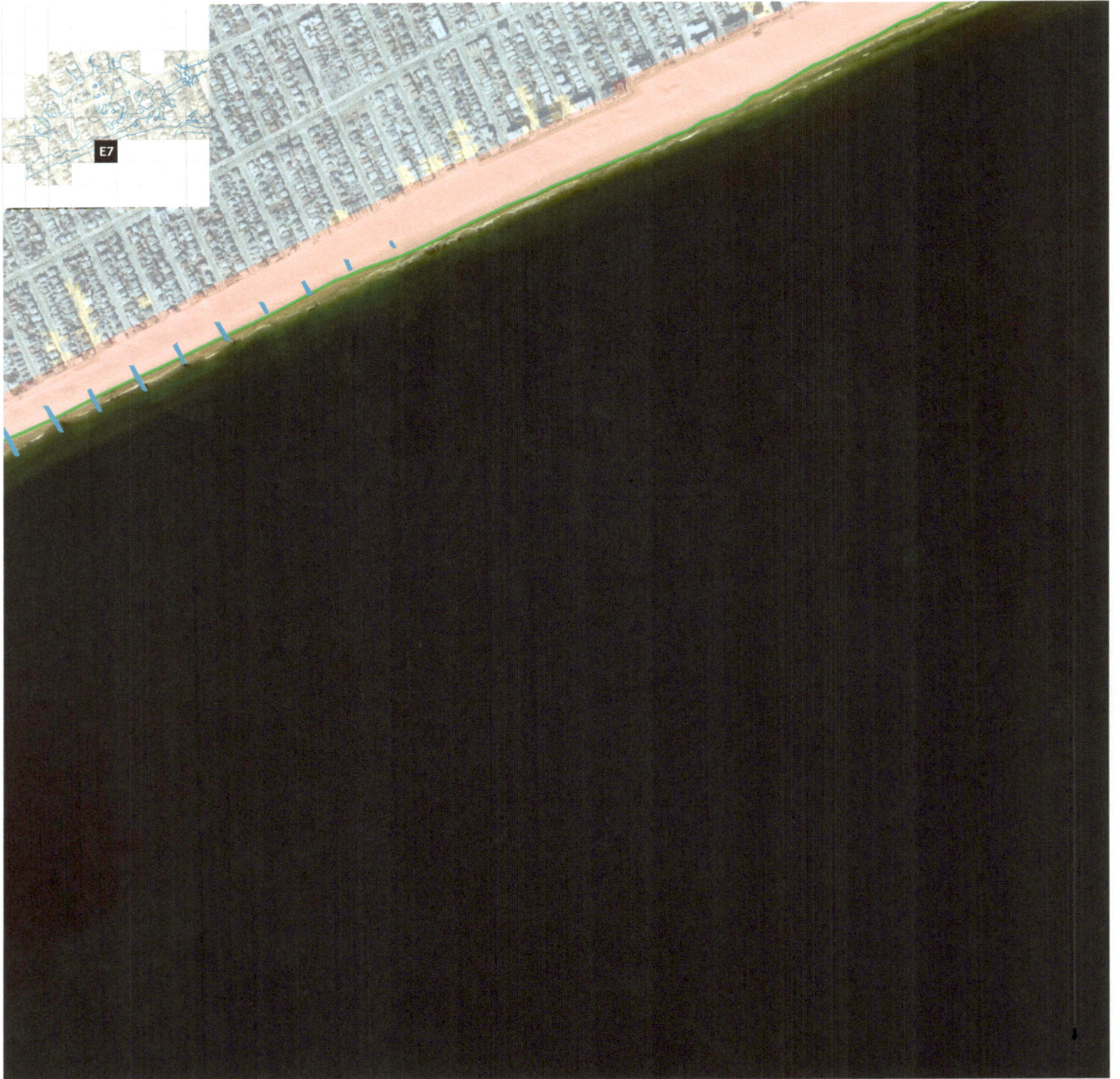

E7

1 1

1 3

1 0

1 1

1 2

1 4

1 3

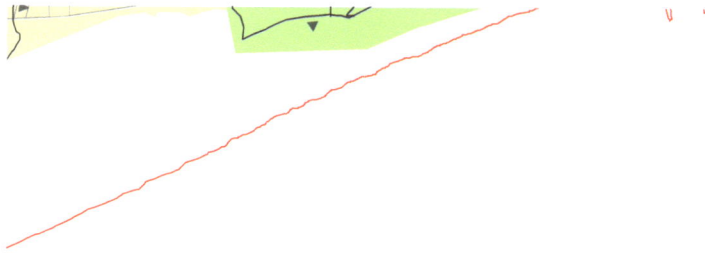

NOTES ON DATA AND SOURCES

Aerial imagery Tiles from ESRI World Imagery map server, accessed October 2013.

Land use GIS data from New York City Department of City Planning, MapPLUTO Release 14v1, May 2014. No land use data for Nassau County was publicly available for download.

Edge condition Coding is compiled from the New York City Department of Environmental Protection's Jamaica Bay Watershed Protection Plan Volume 1, Figure 4.5.1 (Natural and Artificial Shoreline) from October 2007; the National Park Service Inventory of Coastal Engineering Projects in Gateway National Recreation Area from May 1, 2013; and FEMA's Preliminary Digital Flood Insurace Rate Map dataset from December 5, 2013. The shoreline shown is based on the Waterline from this FEMA dataset and manually refined using aerial imagery and NOAA Navigational Chart 12350.

Flood zone Maps shown are FEMA's Preliminary Digital Flood Insurance Rate Maps (DFIRMs) current as of December 5, 2013, accessed from the New York City Digital Flood Insurance Rate Map database. No data was available for Nassau County. Shown in this atlas are Special Flood Hazard Areas VE (pink tone overlaid with aerial) and AE (blue tone overlaid with aerial), as well as Moderate Flood Hazard Areas B/X (yellow tone overlaid with aerial). Also shown are the BFE (numbers overlaid with land use map) and LiMWA (black line and arrows overlaid with land use map).

Zone B/X is defined by FEMA as: Moderate flood hazard areas, labeled Zone B or Zone X (shaded), are the areas between the limits of the base flood and the 0.2-percent-annual-chance (500-year) flood.

Zone AE is defined by FEMA as: Areas subject to inundation by the 1-percent-annual-chance (100-year) flood event. The delineated flood hazard includes wave heights less than three feet.

Zone VE is defined by FEMA as: Areas subject to inundation by the 1-percent-annual-chance (100-year) flood event with additional hazards due to storm-induced velocity wave action. The delineated flood hazard includes wave heights equal to or greater than three feet.

LiMWA is the Limit of Moderate Wave Action, defined by FEMA as the 1.5-foot wave height line. Properties in Zone AE or VE may be affected by waves 1.5 feet or higher. Wave heights as small as 1.5 feet can cause significant damage to structures when constructed without consideration to the coastal hazards.

BFE is the Base Flood Elevation, defined by FEMA as the computed elevation to which floodwater is anticipated to rise during the base flood (1-percent-annual-chance / 100-year flood).

LAND USE

- ONE AND TWO FAMILY BUILDINGS
- MULTIFAMILY WALKUP BUILDINGS
- MULTIFAMILY ELEVATOR BUILDINGS
- MIXED COMMERCIAL / RESIDENTIAL
- COMMERCIAL / OFFICE BUILDINGS
- INDUSTRIAL / MANUFACTURING

- TRANSPORTATION / UTILITY
- PUBLIC FACILITIES AND INSTITUTIONS
- OPEN SPACE
- PARKING FACILITIES
- VACANT LAND
- ALL OTHERS / NO DATA

EDGE CONDITION

- BULKHEAD / SEA WALL
- REVETMENT
- RIPRAP
- BREAKWATER

- JETTY / GROIN
- PIER
- BRIDGE / CAUSEWAY
- SOFT / UNDEFINED

FLOOD ZONE

B/X (SHADED) 0.2% CHANCE ANNUAL / 500-YEAR FLOOD

AE 1% CHANCE ANNUAL / 100-YEAR FLOOD (BFE SHOWN) WITH WAVE HEIGHTS LESS THAN THREE FEET

VE 1% CHANCE ANNUAL / 100-YEAR FLOOD (BFE SHOWN) WITH ADDITIONAL HAZARDS DUE TO STORM-INDUCED VELOCITY WAVE ACTION (WAVE HEIGHTS EQUAL TO OR GREATER THAN THREE FEET)

FEMA LIMIT OF MODERATE WAVE ACTION / BASE FLOOD ELEVATION

SHORELINE

www.ingramcontent.com/pod-product-compliance
Lightning Source LLC
Chambersburg PA
CBHW060809270326
41928CB00002B/34